REINVENTING INVENTION

A **CRAYOLA** GUIDE TO **INNOVATION**

Jennifer Boothroyd

Lerner Publications ◆ Minneapolis

Official Licensed Product

Lerner Publications Company
An imprint of Lerner Publishing Group, Inc.
241 First Avenue North
Minneapolis, MN 55401 USA

For reading levels and more information, look up this title at www.lernerbooks.com.

Main body text set in Mikado a.
Typeface provided by HVD fonts.

Editor: Rebecca Higgins **Designer:** Lindsey Owens

Library of Congress Cataloging-in-Publication Data

Names: Boothroyd, Jennifer, 1972- author.
Title: Reinventing invention : a Crayola guide to innovation / Jennifer Boothroyd.
Description: Minneapolis : Lerner Publications, [2021] | Includes bibliographical references and index. | Audience: Ages 8–12 | Audience: Grades 4–6 | Summary: "This dive into the history of popular and lesser-known inventions is sure to inspire reader curiosity. Untold details behind the invention of the light bulb, the Super Soaker, and more challenge what readers might have heard"– Provided by publisher.
Identifiers: LCCN 2020014669 (print) | LCCN 2020014670 (ebook) | ISBN 9781728403212 (library binding) | ISBN 9781728418575 (ebook)
Subjects: LCSH: Inventions—History—Juvenile literature.
Classification: LCC T15 .B66 2021 (print) | LCC T15 (ebook) | DDC 609—dc23

LC record available at https://lccn.loc.gov/2020014669
LC ebook record available at https://lccn.loc.gov/2020014670

Manufactured in the United States of America
1-48292-48836-8/28/2020

TABLE OF CONTENTS

HOW ARE INVENTIONS MADE?

MOST INVENTION STORIES TELL OF A MIRACULOUS IDEA THAT BECOMES AN OVERNIGHT SUCCESS. But that is rarely the case. Inventions are often the result of improving an existing idea, and failure happens more often than not. Inventors embrace failure and learn from it. Their failed attempts put them on the path to success.

As you read this book, think about how you can push through failure and create new possibilities.

THE LIGHT BULB

THE STORY

In 1879 Thomas Edison invented a light bulb. His light bulb used electricity to heat a filament inside a glass bulb. When heated, the filament created light. Soon Edison's light bulbs were used in homes and businesses across the United States of America.

Including his light bulb, Edison patented 1,093 of his inventions.

Thomas Edison didn't invent the first light bulb. Decades before Edison, inventors were making their own light bulbs. Edison is known for his improvement of the light bulb. He and his assistants tested over six thousand filaments to create a dependable and affordable model. Edison showed people that his bulbs were practical and safe for use. More than one hundred years later, people continue to improve the light bulb. LED light bulbs use less energy than previous models.

BE AN INVENTOR

Edison may not have invented the light bulb, but his improvements to it had a lasting impact. Look closer at the things you see every day from your school supplies to the technology you use. What is working with these items, and what isn't? How can you fix what isn't working?

HOLLOW FLASHLIGHT

Ann Makosinski had a friend in the Philippines who was struggling to study. Her home didn't have electricity, and she didn't have enough light to read her textbooks. Ann wanted to help. So she created the Hollow Flashlight, a device powered by renewable energy.

Ann's advice to inventors is to work on your creation a little bit every day.

A curious kid, Ann had always liked to tinker with objects. She had been interested in renewable energy sources since middle school. Ann's flashlight absorbs body heat from a person's hand and converts it to light. It took many tries to ensure the flashlight both produced enough power and stayed safe to use. She was sixteen years old when her invention won the Google Science Fair in 2013.

TINKER
/TINK-er/
verb
to adjust, repair, disassemble, or invent something. Tinkering generally follows from curiosity about an object or idea.

THE TELEPHONE

THE STORY

Alexander Graham Bell was determined to create the telephone. In March of 1876, he and his assistant, Thomas Watson, tried again. Bell carefully spoke into the device. "Mr. Watson, come here. I need you." Watson ran in from the next room. It worked! Bell had invented the first telephone.

Alexander Graham Bell started inventing at the age of eleven and continued for the rest of his life.

Alexander Graham Bell was inspired by inventions that sent sounds using electricity. He wanted to talk to someone in a similar way. But Bell wasn't the only person with the idea. He found himself in a race against other inventors, each trying to create a telephone. Bell won the race on February 14, 1876, when he submitted his patent a couple of hours before another inventor. But Bell's telephone didn't work. Bell and Watson kept adjusting, and on March 10, 1876, it finally worked. Bell's invention became the talk of the town.

Early telephones, such as Bell's telephone (*right*), led to the development of the modern-day smartphone.

SUPER SOAKER

THE STORY

The Super Soaker has been a childhood favorite for years. This special squirt gun uses compressed air to shoot a large amount of water over a long distance. Lonnie G. Johnson invented the Super Soaker in 1982 and sold millions. It was an instant success.

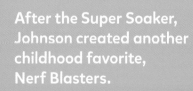

After the Super Soaker, Johnson created another childhood favorite, Nerf Blasters.

Johnson, a rocket scientist for NASA, was tinkering at home. He was trying to create a new type of heat pump. When it accidentally shot water across the room, he thought it would make a great squirt gun. Johnson made a prototype for his daughter. It became a popular toy around the neighborhood. He filed for a patent and worked to get a toy company to produce it. His perseverance paid off, and his squirt gun finally made it to store shelves in 1990. The Super Soaker was inducted into the National Toy Hall of Fame in 2015.

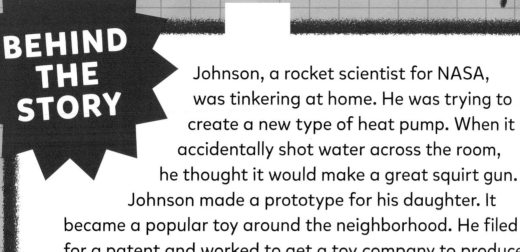

PERSEVERANCE

/ˈpərsəˈvirəns/

noun

a determined focus to reach a goal regardless of obstacles or difficulties

DUSTLESS CHALK

Edwin Binney and Harold Smith specialized in colorful pigments. They invented special crayons to mark their shipments to customers. Eventually crayons became the main part of their business. Together they created the company Binney & Smith, which sold Crayola brand products.

THE STORY

Binney (*left*) and Smith (*right*) started off by creating pigments that made barns red and tires black.

BEHIND THE STORY

Binney and Smith didn't invent the first crayons, but they developed crayons that were safe and affordable. And crayons weren't even the first or only school supply the partners improved. Binney's wife, Alice, was a teacher and noticed that kids were getting sick from using chalk. The chalk created a lot of dust that kids would breathe in. Binney and Smith solved the problem by creating dustless chalk in 1902. Their business expanded from there to include more colorful products.

When Binney and Smith visited schools to demonstrate their dustless chalk, they saw the need for more dependable crayons. Their eight-pack of crayons came out in 1903.

TRADE **CRAYOLA** MARK

GOLD MEDAL

EIGHT COLORS

SCHOOL CRAYONS

FOR EDUCATIONAL COLOR WORK.

MANUFACTURED BY
BINNEY & SMITH CO.
NEW YORK. PARIS.

iPOD

THE STORY

Before the year 2000, many people listened to music on portable CD players. Digital music players existed, but they were hard to use. That all changed in 2001 when Steve Jobs presented his latest invention, the iPod. This portable music player could digitally store about one thousand songs, and it was easy to use. By April 2007, Apple had sold one hundred million iPods worldwide.

Now Playing
9 of 13
Just Feel Better
Santana
All That I Am
3:30   -0:49

Jobs was often mistaken as the sole inventor for Apple.

Fadell went on to help Apple invent the iPhone.

In 1999 Tony Fadell was working on a digital music player of his own. But he didn't have the money to develop it. Apple hired Fadell to lead the team that would develop the iPod. After the iPod was released, a company accused Apple of stealing their idea. It turned out that a man named Kane Kramer had filed the original patent for a portable digital music player in 1979. But the player couldn't be made with 1970s technology, so when the patent expired in 1988, any inventor could use the idea.

NYSTATIN

THE STORY

Severe skin infections caused by fungus used to be incurable. In 1950 scientists Rachel Fuller Brown and Elizabeth Lee Hazen developed Nystatin, the first successful antifungal medicine. It has greatly reduced the number of severe cases of fungal infections all over the world.

Nystatin, invented by Hazen (*left*) and Brown (*right*), is still used to treat people.

Brown and Hazen were scientists working for the New York Department of Health. Their job was to find a natural substance that would kill fungus. But their team had an extra challenge. Their labs were over 100 miles (161 km) apart. When Hazen found promising substances in soil, she mailed a sample to Brown. Brown separated the substance from the soil and mailed it back to Hazen. Then Hazen tested whether the substance killed fungus. After many tests, they finally discovered Nystatin.

Brown and Hazen studied soil samples for years before inventing Nystatin.

BE AN INVENTOR

By working together, Brown and Hazen invented Nystatin. Who is someone that you like to work with? Talk to that person and see what you are both interested in. Then brainstorm inventions based on your shared interest.

BLOOD BANKS

Whole blood can be stored only a week before spoiling. Hospitals struggled to keep enough fresh blood for patients in need of transfusions. In 1939 Dr. Charles Drew invented a way to preserve blood plasma. Plasma could be stored for months in special centers called blood banks and shipped to other places when needed. During World War II (1939–1945), Drew directed blood collection programs that saved many injured soldiers.

Drew discovered how to preserve blood while still in medical school.

In 1940 Drew led the Blood for Britain project. Over fourteen thousand pints of blood were donated in the United States, preserved in blood banks, and sent to British hospitals. The next year, Drew directed the American Red Cross blood bank. He organized the collection of blood for use in the United States. He introduced blood donation trucks, later called bloodmobiles, to make it easier for donors to find a place to donate blood. In addition to saving lives, Drew became the first African American examiner on the American Board of Surgery.

Blood banks have saved millions of lives.

PENICILLIN

After a vacation, Dr. Alexander Fleming returned to his lab to find mold growing on a dirty lab dish. He noticed that the mold had stopped bacteria from growing on the dish. Fleming had accidentally discovered penicillin. It became an important medicine to treat infections caused by bacteria.

Fleming was experimenting with the flu virus when he discovered penicillin.

But he didn't know what to do next. A decade later, Dr. Howard Florey read about Fleming's discovery. He and his team of scientists learned how to separate penicillin from the mold. They also identified molds that made larger amounts of penicillin. Finally, they convinced chemical companies to start making penicillin into medicine. The medicine has saved millions of lives.

Penicillin was first used in 1942.

200,000 UNITS
SOLTABS
CRYSTALLINE PENICILLIN G
POTASSIUM SALT
CSC
20 CC. SIZE   LIST NO. 702
FOR PARENTERAL ADMINISTRATION.
CAUTION: To be dispensed only by or on the prescription of a physician or dentist. FOR DIRECTIONS SEE ENCLOSED LEAFLET
C.S.C. Pharmaceuticals
A DIVISION OF COMMERCIAL SOLVENTS CORPORATION
NEW YORK 17, N.Y., U.S.A.

WHEN IN SOLUTION REFRIGERATE

SAFETY HOOD

THE STORY

In 1916 an explosion trapped workers in a tunnel. Rescuers couldn't reach the workers because of the smoke and toxic gas. Garrett Morgan grabbed his invention, the safety hood, and raced to the accident. Thanks to the safety hood, he safely entered the tunnel and saved some of the workers.

Morgan continued solving problems after inventing the safety hood. He prevented car accidents by creating an early version of the stoplight.

BE AN INVENTOR

Morgan's invention protected people from smoke. What problems do you see or hear others talking about? How might you solve this problem?

BEHIND THE STORY

Morgan invented the safety hood in 1912. He had been inspired by seeing an elephant stick its trunk under a circus tent wall to get some fresh air. The canvas hood had a glass window to see through and a long hose that ran from the bottom of the hood to a sponge that could filter smoke and toxic gas. Hundreds of fire departments across the country bought his invention. Morgan's mask inspired the gas mask that saved soldiers from chemical attacks in World War I (1914–1918).

The lifesaving safety hood led to more equipment for firefighters.

SOIL WATER STORAGE

In 2015 a drought in South Africa threatened crop harvests. But teenager Kiara Nirghin had a plan to help struggling farmers. Through her research, she developed a biodegradable gel that holds water. When planted with crops, it releases water to help plants survive.

Nirghin presents her invention at the 2016 Google Science Fair.

Nirghin had always been curious about chemistry, and she enjoyed doing research. She knew there were gels designed to hold moisture, but these gels were expensive and unhealthy for plants and animals. She needed to find a cheap and natural alternative. Her research led her to orange peels and avocado skins. Through trial and error, she experimented with different combinations until she created a mixture that worked better than other gels. Nirghin won the 2016 Google Science Fair for her invention.

TRIAL AND ERROR
/ˈtraɪ(ə)l/ /æn(d)/ /ˈɛrər/
noun
succeeding by making improvements after repeatedly trying and failing

KID INVENTORS

Louis Braille, fifteen years old, 1824

Louis Braille developed braille, a system for reading and writing for people who are visually impaired. The characters in braille are raised dots that represent letters and numbers. People use their fingers to feel the different characters. Braille has been translated into languages all over the world.

Sarah Buckel, fourteen years old, 2006

Sarah Buckel wanted an easier way to decorate her locker. The stickers she used were too hard to get off at the end of the school year. With her dad's help, she created magnetic wallpaper for metal lockers. Sarah received a patent for her invention and sold millions of magnetic stickers.

Kenneth Shinozuka, fifteen years old, 2014

Kenneth Shinozuka created his wearable sensors to help keep his grandfather safe. His grandfather suffered from Alzheimer's and would leave the house in the middle of the night. The sensors on his socks let a caregiver know when he was out of bed. Kenneth started the company SensaRx to sell his invention.

Alaina Gassler, fourteen years old, 2019

Alaina Gassler invented a system that eliminates blind spots in cars. The system makes a windshield's side supports seem invisible. This prevents accidents that may happen when the supports block a driver's view. Her invention has won awards, but she wants to keep improving the technology used in her prototype.

GLOSSARY

compressed: squeezed into less space

filament: a fine wire that gives off light when connected to electricity

infection: a disease caused by germs entering parts of the body

invention: an idea or solution created through innovative thinking

patent: a government document that gives a person or company the right to use or make an invention for a certain amount of time

prototype: a first working model of an invention

technology: methods and devices that are used to do tasks

LEARN MORE

Beattie, Rob. *Invent It! Turn Your Small Idea into the World's Next Great Invention*. New York: Sterling Children's Books, 2017.

iKids
https://inventivekids.com/

Krasner, Barbara. *Great Invention Fails*. Minneapolis: Lerner Publications, 2020.

Lemelson Center for the Study of Invention and Innovation: Spark Lab
https://invention.si.edu/try/sparklab

National Park Service: Thomas Edison Online Games
https://www.nps.gov/edis/learn/education/onlinegames.htm

Turner, Matt. *Genius Transportation Inventions: From the Wheel to Spacecraft*. Minneapolis: Hungry Tomato, 2018.

INDEX

PHOTO ACKNOWLEDGMENTS

Image credits: The_Pixel/Shutterstock.com, p. 1 (background); fizkes/ Shutterstock.com, p. 5 (top); Monkey Business Images/Shutterstock.com, p. 5 (bottom); Library of Congress (LC-USZ62 98066), p. 6; daniiD/Shutterstock .com, p. 7; Joern Pollex/Getty Images for Greentech Festival/Getty Images, p. 8; ansonsaw/E+/Getty Images, p. 9; Library of Congress (LC-H25- 11186-F), p. 10; Science & Society Picture Library/Getty Images, p. 11; Thomas S. England/The LIFE Images Collection/Getty Images, p. 12; Tom Wang/Shutterstock.com, p. 13; Courtesy of Crayola, pp. 14 (all), 15; Kim Kulish/Corbis/Getty Images, p. 16; dpa/ Alamy Stock Photo, p. 16; Photo Researchers/Alamy Stock Photo, p. 18; Sodel Vladyslav/Shutterstock.com, p. 19; Science History Images/Alamy Stock Photo, p. 20; Pressmaster/Shutterstock.com, p. 21; Walter Cicchetti/Shutterstock .com, p. 23; Fotosearch/Getty Images, p. 24; Gorgev/Shutterstock.com, p. 25; Deon Raath/Foto24/Gallo Images/Getty Images, p. 26; Bohdan Lytvynenko/ Shutterstock.com, p. 27; Photo by Apic/Getty Images, p. 28; Jemal Countess// Getty Images, p. 29.